RAINER MARIA RILKE

THE SONNETS TO ORPHEUS

Translated by David Cook

Andrew

All good wishes

David

Nothing but a Breath

Nichts als ein Atemzug... Rainer Maria Rilke

The double beat of the heart
pulse of the dance.
Breathing's two-step
binding ghost and spirit
what is gone to what is present.
The rhythm of the earth
phases of absence and abundance.
These,
like lovers who strengthen their bond
by being apart
or brothers who again and again
quarrel and come back together,
are the poles of hoped for renewal.

In the end
there was no tug of relatedness
just the counterweight of his past
and astonished return
to a world that was younger than before.

And there grew in him
a tender regard
for all those, carelessly ventured,
vulnerable as fledgling sparrows,
who bear their suffering alone.

Somehow we worry about his dying.

Still he continues to sing.

David Cook, November 2011

RAINER MARIA RILKE

THE SONNETS TO ORPHEUS

Translated by David Cook

 *redcliffe*

First published in 2012 by Redcliffe Press Ltd.,
81g Pembroke Road, Bristol BS8 3EA
www.redcliffepress.co.uk
e: info@redcliffepress.co.uk
tel: 0117 973 7207

ISBN 978-1-908326-14-0

British Library Cataloguing-in-Publication Data
A catalogue record for this book is available from the British Library

Design and typesetting by Stephen Morris www.stephen-morris.co.uk
Printed and bound by MPG Books Ltd, Bodmin, Cornwall

Contents

Preface

I worked as a consultant psychiatrist, predominantly in Bristol, between 1982 and 2011. My interest in Rilke grew with my appreciation of his exceptional sensitivity to everything that impinged on him and his vision of the possibility of a deep interconnectedness between nature and human beings. Despite this, he had a recurring need for solitude as a means of preserving his fragile sense of himself. Love above all was problematic to him. He did however build up an extraordinary network of devoted friends and admirers who helped sustain him through his numerous personal crises.

His unwavering sense of the mystery and holiness of life was an inspiration to me during my time as a psychiatrist, because I always felt that medical and social science were, by themselves, unequal to the task of helping people with seriously troubled lives.

The purpose of these translations is to provide an accessible and idiomatic English version of *The Sonnets to Orpheus*, while remaining faithful to the original German. After some deliberation I decided not to include the German text in this edition because I am neither a linguist nor a scholar. However, I parsed every sentence of these poems in my effort to understand what Rilke was saying and I have done all that I can to render them in a spare and fluent English. I hope I have communicated some of my feeling of wonder and delight.

I have also included my translation of *Sketches from Two Winter Evenings*, written in 1924, because, as well as being a great poem, it provides a stunning account of the origins of Rilke's muse-inspired poetry.

David Cook

Introduction

Despite his vision of the inter-relatedness of living things and the healing power of nature, Rilke also had a sense of the abysses of unique experience which separate us and make intimacy so difficult. In his own life, though he yearned for love, he repeatedly became disappointed or felt trapped, and would move away into the solitude of his poetic calling. Princess Marie von Thurn und Taxis-Hohenlohe, in her unfailingly sympathetic memoir of Rilke, put it thus, 'his jealous god would not share him'. Towards the end of his life, he came to accept that his muse would always be an unattainable ideal. He also realised that in order to practise his art as a poet he would have to renounce the possibility of any kind of conjugal happiness, and in achieving this understanding the archetypal figure of Orpheus stood as exemplar. 'Be dead forever in Eurydice, and rise more strongly praising…'

The story of how *The Sonnets to Orpheus* were written is well known but it remains remarkable for all that. A number of unconnected events came together to facilitate a poetic outpouring over three weeks in February 1922. This intense period of creativity resulted in the completion of the *Duino Elegies*, the project begun ten years earlier and regarded by Rilke as his supreme task as a poet, and at the same time the writing of *The Sonnets to Orpheus*, an occurrence which took him completely by surprise.

In May 1921, Rilke had been living in Switzerland for over a year but then became homeless. His lover, Baladine Klossowska (called Merline by Rilke), visited in June while he was staying at Hôtel Château Bellevue in Sierre, and together they found an isolated thirteenth-century tower,

Château de Muzot, on the outskirts of Sierre. After compli-
cated negotiations, the Château was leased for him by one of
his patrons, Werner Reinhart. When it later came up for sale,
Reinhart bought it outright. Rilke moved in with Merline
and they lived there together for more than three months. In
early November she left to be with her two young sons in
Berlin. Some time before leaving she had bought a postcard
reproduction of a drawing by the Venetian artist Cima de
Conegliana (1459-1517) depicting Orpheus under a tree
playing a viol while animals listened. She had pinned this
above Rilke's writing desk and soon after her departure he
noted in a letter that she had left it behind, but he kept it
anyway.

Château de Muzot was the nearest Rilke came to having a
home of his own during his adult life and he lived there until
he became too ill to live alone, although he spent seven months
in Paris at the beginning of 1925. His letters towards the end
of 1921 indicate that he had begun to feel settled for the first
time in years and that he was preparing for a period of
solitude and concentration in order to try and finish the
Duino Elegies.

Also at this time, he resumed a correspondence with
Gertrud Ouckama Knoop, the widow of his friend Gerhard,
whose younger daughter had died of leukaemia in 1919 at
the age of nineteen. The daughter, Vera, had been a friend of
Rilke's daughter Ruth in Munich before the War, and he had
met her there and seen her dance. In a letter to Gertrud
dated 26th November 1921, Rilke asked Gertrud if she
would send him some little thing that was dear to Vera and
on 1st January 1922 Rilke received from Gertrud, a journal
kept by Vera of the last weeks before her death. In a letter of
acknowledgement he writes of its enormous impact on him:

'How completely she experienced with all her being, those things to which these memorials of her agony bear such deep and irrevocable witness, – and how marvellous, how unique, how incomparable a human being is! For when everything should have been consumed, suddenly there rose up enough for a whole life: a great flood of light in her heart, and in it appeared, shining, the two extremes of her understanding: that pain is a mistake, a blind misapprehension of the body driving its wedge between heaven and earth, when they are one; and on the other hand, the oneness of her wide-open heart with the living everlasting world…' He concludes the letter, 'But for me it has come as an immense obligation to my innermost self and (even if I only attain it from afar) to my serenity, that I am allowed, on the first evening of a new year, to take these pages into my possession.'

And then in February, the storm of creativity blew through him. He wrote the first part of *The Sonnets to Orpheus* between 2nd and 5th February and wrote to Gertrud Ouckama Knoop on the 7th and again on the 9th telling her about them, sending copies and detailing minor amendments in the second letter. He knew immediately that he wanted to dedicate them to Vera and asked Gertrud to agree a form of words.

There then followed the long hoped for work on the *Duino Elegies*, so that on 11th February he was able to write jubilantly to Princess Marie that he had completed the work which belatedly took the form of ten elegies. He also wrote to Lou Andreas-Salomé telling her of the breakthrough. However, there followed further revisions so that although the number remained at ten, the published Fifth Elegy was written a few days after the letters had been sent. In the work's final form, the Fifth, Seventh, and Eighth Elegies were written entirely at Muzot, together with most of the Ninth and Tenth. At some time during the completion of the Elegies, Rilke also wrote a lengthy prose fragment, unpublished in his lifetime, but now known as the 'Worker Letter'. After writing the Fifth Elegy, he wrote the second part of *The Sonnets to Orpheus*, and in a letter to Lou Andreas-Salomé on 20th February told her of the completion of the Elegies and that he was arranging a second group of *The Sonnets to Orpheus*.

That there are connections between the *Duino Elegies* and *The Sonnets to Orpheus* is almost self-evident, given the circumstances of their creation. However, they also stand alone as coherent achievements. This is not the place to discuss the relationship between the two works in any detail and I will limit myself to two observations. The Angels of the *Duino Elegies* and the Orpheus of the *Sonnets* provide points of contact with a timeless realm of which humanity is largely unaware. Also the Angels are remote, austere and even forbidding figures, while Orpheus, though a god, is recognizably a friend to man.

Rilke continued to live at Château de Muzot and wrote a large number of poems in German as well as several hundred short poems in French. He spent seven months in Paris at the beginning of 1925, meeting with many French writers and old friends including Merline. His health deteriorated over some years but he was diagnosed as suffering from leukaemia only weeks before his death in December 1926.

THE SONNETS TO ORPHEUS

Written as a memorial for
Vera Ouckama Knoop

Château de Muzot, February 1922

Part One

I,1

A tree sprang up! O pure and lofty yearning!
O Orpheus sings! O tall tree in the ear!
And all was silent. Yet in the holding back,
from hint and secret stirring something was born.

Beasts of the stillness crowded the wilderness
leaving behind in the forest their lairs and dens,
and so it happened that it was neither cunning
nor fearfulness, but only that they listened

that quietened them. The growls and shrieks
and bellows seemed to grow small inside them:
and there, where there had been so little shelter

to hold such large devotion, no sanctuary
with trembling porch to enter, you
built for them a temple in the ear.

I,2

And she was just a girl and she appeared
out of this simple joy of lyre and song
and shone out brightly through her springtime bloom
and made herself a bed within my ear.

And slept in me. And all things were her sleep:
trees that had stirred my wonder, those
sensed distances, the rough meadows
and each amazement that had touched my heart.

She slept the world. O singing God,
how did you so perfect her that her first wish
was not to be awake? She rose and slept.

Where is her death? O will you ever re-invent
this theme, before your song is ended? –
Where does she fall from me? … A girl almost …

I,3

A god can do it. But tell me how a man
shall follow him across the narrow lyre.
His mind is discord. At the heart's crossed
vessels there stands no temple to Apollo.

Song, as you instruct, is not desire,
not the pursuit of what in the end may be caught.
Song is being. A slight thing for a god.
But when shall we just be? And when will he

entrust us with the earth and with the stars?
That you love, young poet, is not the vital thing,
even if your voice forces open your mouth.

Learn to forget first song. Soon it will pass.
Truth to be sung requires a different breath.
A breath on nothing. A stirring in the god. A wind.

I,4

O you who are so tender, step sometimes
into the path of the disdainful god;
allow his breath to break across your cheeks
and stir behind you as it eddies back.

O you who are so happy, you who are whole,
you who shine with young untarnished hearts –
bows for the arrows, targets for their flight:
though tear-stained may your smiles win through for ever.

But do not be afraid to suffer, let the weight fall
into the untold vastness of the Earth,
into the heavy mountains, the heavy seas.

Even the trees you planted when you were children
have grown toward their deaths, cannot be held back.
And yet there are the breezes… there are the spaces…

I,5

Set up no stone. Just cultivate the rose
to flower each year as a sign.
For it is Orpheus. His changing form
in this and that. We do not need to find

another name. We know for sure it is him
whenever there is song. He comes and goes.
And don't we sense him near for a day or two
after the roses have faded in their bowl?

O how he must withdraw for you to grasp it!
And all the while he knew that he would leave.
But just as his word transcends the here and now,

so he is there already, where you cannot go.
You shall not force his hands to the lyre's strings
and he obeys even as he steps across.

I,6

Is this where he's at home? No, his wide nature
has grown from both great realms,
and he who travels past the willow's roots
may be as skilful plaiting the willow's branches.

If you're for bed, remember not to leave
any bread or milk on the table; it attracts the dead.
But may he, the master of dreams, mix
beneath the eyelids of the sleeping

their presences with everything perceived;
for him the enchantment of fumitory and rue
is just as real as clear relatedness.

Nothing can harm his numinous images;
whether they come from graves, whether from houses,
he praises them; finger ring, bracelet and jug.

I,7

To praise is the task! And one appointed to praise
came forth like ore out of the silent
stone. His heart, O earthly press,
filled with eternal wine for the good of mankind.

Nor does his voice weaken at the dusty work
when the godlike manner is on him.
All becomes vineyard, all becomes grape,
turning to ripeness in his benevolent South.

Not decay in the tombs of kings
nor a shadow that falls from the gods
have betrayed him into false piety.

He is one of the resolute messengers,
one who still travels beyond the gates of the dead,
carrying bowls of fruit worthy of praise.

I,8

Only in the space made by praising, is grief
allowed to occur, the nymph of the weeping spring
watches over our sorrowful tears
that they be clear right down to the rock

on which gateways and altars are raised. –
See, how across her still shoulders
dawns the feeling that perhaps it is she
who is youngest of the sisters of the heart.

Rejoicing knows, and longing acknowledges faults,
it is only sorrow that learns; with a girl's hands
night after night, she tells over ancient wrongs.

Yet suddenly, awkward and untaught,
she holds up our voice as stars
into the darkened sky, unclouded by her breath.

I,9

Only one who has lifted his lyre
among the shades,
is able to restore
unending ancestral praise.

Only one who has eaten poppies
with the dead,
will not forget
the rarest melodies.

Often the reflection in a pond
breaks up as we look.
Retain the image.

Only in the double realm
do voices become
eternal and mild.

I,10

You, who never wholly left my mind,
I greet, antique sarcophagi,
which the Roman waters of my youth
flowed through like a wandering song.

Or the open ones, like the eyes
of a happy watchful shepherd,
– filled with stillness and flowering nettle,
from which delighted butterflies take flight.

I greet all those who have cast off indecision,
and opened their mouths again
after long silence, knowing what that means.

Do we know, friends, or do we not?
These two, certainty and doubt,
etch the passing hours on the human face.

I,11

Search the sky. Is there no constellation called 'Rider'?
For this proud beast is strangely impressed
on us. And a second, the one
who speeds and slows him, and whom he carries.

Isn't it just like this, spurred on and then reined back,
the sinewy nature of our being?
Straight ahead, then turning. At a touch, assent.
New horizons. Then the two are one.

But are they? Or do they rather
each intend the way they choose together?
Of course table and pasture utterly divide them.

Even the starry union is deceptive.
And yet let us be happy for a little while,
having faith in the image. That in the end is enough.

I,12

Hail to the spirit able to unite us;
for we do surely live by images.
And so with little steps the clock advances
beside our actual undivided day.

Without an understanding of our true place,
we act out of a real relatedness.
Antennae feel for antennae
and the empty spaces carry

high tension. O music of begetting!
Is it not through your everyday pursuits
that the greater forces are deflected from you?

Even though the farmer toils and troubles,
to where the seed is turning into summer
he never reaches. This the earth gives.

I,13

Ripe apple, pear, banana,
gooseberry… all these bring
death and life into the mouth… I look for…
read it in the face of a child who

is tasting them. This comes from far-away.
Do you have a sense of what is strange arriving?
Where otherwise were words, now come discoveries,
free and startled out of the fruit's flesh.

Consider what it is that 'apple' names.
This sweetness, which first collects itself,
so that through softly stirring taste

we may become clear, awake, transparent,
complex, sunny, earthy, local – :
O deftness, touch, delight – , astonishment.

I,14

We carry with us always, flower, vine-leaf, fruit.
They do not only speak the speech of the year.
Out of the darkness rises a bright display
that has upon it, perhaps, a jealous gleam

of the possessive dead who throng the soil.
What do we know about their part in this?
Long has it been the practice to plough back
all surplus crops into the weakened earth.

Now only ask this question: do they do it gladly?
Do these round fruit, the work of heavy slaves,
thrust upward willingly to us their masters?

Or is it they, not we who are the masters,
who sleep beside the root and from their plenty
grant us this mixture of silent power and kisses?

I,15

Let's see…, that taste of…, no, it's gone already,
… Just a snatch of melody, a stamping, a humming –
girls, it's warm, girls, it's subtle,
please dance the taste of the many fruit you've known.

Dance the orange. Who can forget how,
drowning in its own juice, it nevertheless fights
against the sweetness. You've eaten it
and had it melt deliciously into you.

Dance the orange. Find a southern landscape
in yourself, so that the fruit will ripen
in warmer air. It glows, peel back

scent on scent. Know the relationship
between the chaste containing rind
and the juice with which so wantonly it's filled.

I,16

You, my loyal friend are lonely, because…
it is we who with words and gestures
bit by bit lay claim to the world,
though perhaps at its weakest, most treacherous places.

Who, for example, can point a finger at a smell?
And yet of the unseen powers that threaten us
you feel so many… you know the dead,
you grow afraid at the magician's patter.

So now let us agree to bear together
the patchwork and the pieces as though it were the whole.
To help you will be difficult. Above all

do not plant me in your heart. I should grow too fast.
But I will guide my master's hand and say:
here. May I commend Esau in his pelt.

I,17

Deepest of all the old one,
gnarled root of everything,
buried origin,
which they have never seen.

Helmet and hunting horn,
wisdom of the elders,
men in their rivalries,
women like lutes…

branch caught on branch,
none wholly free…
One perhaps! O climb…

All of them will break.
At last the highest one
bends into a lyre.

I,18

Do you hear the new age, Lord,
shaking and throbbing?
Also the messengers,
those who proclaim it.

Hearing is injured
in the commotion,
and yet the deft machine
forces our praise.

See, then, the engine:
how violently it labours,
and at the same time, how we are weakened.

Since its power is given by us,
let it, without passion,
be driven and serve.

I,19

Even the world dissolves
like billowing cloud,
all things achieved
return to their beginnings.

Beyond change and clamour,
wider and freer,
cast your sustaining song,
god with a lyre.

We find pain hard to bear
or learn love's teaching,
and death's estrangement

is unremitting.
Only divine song
heals and affirms.

I,20

But to you, master, what shall I dedicate to you
who taught the creatures to listen?
My memory of a Spring day,
evening, in Russia – , a horse…

Across from the village came a white horse by himself,
on one front fetlock a tether,
to spend the night alone up on the meadows;
how the tangled mane beat

against his neck in time with his high spirit,
with his rough hampered gallop.
How that steed's blood leapt!

O yes, he felt the spaces beckon!
He neighed and listened – , thus was your song cycle
fulfilled in him.

His image – this I dedicate.

I,21

Spring has come round again. The earth
is like a child who knows her poems by heart,
many, very many . . . for the effort
of long study she gets the prize.

Her teacher was strict. We liked the white
in the old man's beard.
Now we are allowed to ask what the green,
what the blue means: she knows, she knows!

Earth, happy and free, play now
with the children. We want to possess you,
happy earth. And the happiest will do so.

O, what the teacher taught her, the many lessons,
and what is forever in roots
and long intricate stems: she sings, she sings!

I,22

We are the unswerving.
But time's stride
is a trifle compared with
things lasting for ever.

All haste
will be outdistanced;
for what endures
is first laid down in us.

Boys, set your young hearts
neither on swiftness
nor winged flight.

All things are grounded in rest:
darkness and light,
blossom and book.

I,23

No, not until later, after the flock
has stopped taking off into the sky
for its own sake,
self-absorbed

and from afar,
like an arrow pointing,
the wind's darling,
assured, supple, fleet, –

but rather when some pure question
annuls the boyish pride
in new machines,

will one propelled by victory
toward the distant truth,
then be that lonely, be that soaring flight.

I,24

Should we renounce our age-old allegiance
to the undemonstrative gods, because hard steel,
which we have laboriously fashioned, cannot know them,
or should we relent and search for them on a map?

These mighty friends who bear away our dead
have never slowed us, nowhere touched our wheels.
We have moved our celebrations further off
and always outdistance their careful

messengers. Lonelier now, wholly dependent
on one another, yet without mutual understanding,
we no longer make our way at a leisurely pace

but move on straight ahead. Only in furnaces do fires
still burn, raising hammers that grow ever bigger.
And we meanwhile lose strength like long-distance swimmers.

I,25

But now you, known to me as one knows
a nameless flower, you, forcibly taken;
let me once again remember and proclaim you,
beautiful companion of the undefeated cry.

A dancer first, who suddenly, her body full of lapses,
stopped, as though her youth had turned to bronze;
she suffered and listened – then from the higher powers
music fell into her altered heart.

Illness was near. Already possessed by shadows
her blood became darker, then as if
the danger had passed, some natural strength returned.

But again and again, darkness and ruin broke in with
their mortal gleam. After some dreadful throbbing
the blood went in through the desolate open door.

I,26

Once again I honour you, master, you still making music
until the end; so that when the shrieking horde of Maenads
seized you, your self-possession reached beyond the din
and from their midst was heard your glorious song.

None was there who could break your head or lyre,
much though they wrestled and raged; and even the sharpest
of stones that were hurled at your heart
became smooth and gifted with hearing at your merest touch.

You were hunted out of revenge and finally shattered,
but your sound lingered on in the lions and rocks,
in the trees and birds. And there you sing still.

O you, our lost god! Our never forgotten guide!
In the end it is only because hatred tore you to pieces
that we have learnt to attend, and to speak of nature.

Part Two

II,1

Breathing, you invisible poem!
Again and again I trade
with the pure replenishing void. Counterweight
against whom rhythmically I beat.

Single wave, whose
swelling sea I am;
you, least of all possible seas, –
a breath won from the air.

How many parts of space have already
been within me? Often a wind
is like my own son.

Do you know me, sky, still full of places once mine?
You, who were then the smooth bark,
round limb and leaf of my words.

II,2

Sometimes a sheet of paper near at hand
captures by chance the authentic stroke of a Master,
and so it is with mirrors when they accept
girls' precious fleeting smiles

as they breathe in the morning air alone,
or vie with the brilliancy of lights at nightfall.
And later, across their warm vivacious faces
a ghost may flit of that which they once were.

What do eyes which have been searching a long time
see in the embers of a sinking fire?
Glimpses of a former life now past recall.

O earth, who can reckon your losses?
Only one undaunted, who with a steady voice
can sing the heart, the fullness that it bears.

II,3

Mirrors: no one yet has knowingly said
what you must be in your depths.
You, like the airy holes in sieves,
make up the intervals in time.

You, the prodigals of empty halls –
when twilight comes, wide as the woods…
then the chandelier becomes an antlered stag
at bay beyond your pristine surfaces.

Sometimes you are full of pictures.
A few have blazed right into you –
while others you've sent shyly past.

But the loveliest of all will linger – until
the freed Narcissus has found his way
into her doubting cheeks over there in you.

II,4

And here we have the creature, which is not.
But they did not allow this, and as it happens
– his gait and bearing, his arched neck,
even the light in his eyes – they loved it all.

Yet truly he was not. But because they loved him
the beast was seen. And always they made room.
And in that space, empty and unbounded,
he raised an elegant head but scarcely fought

for his existence. They fed him make-believe grain
so as to give him strength to struggle free.
This gave the beast such power

that out of his own forehead he grew a horn. A single horn.
Then pure white to a young girl he came near,
and was in her silver mirror and in her.

II,5

Flower-muscle that opens out the meadow morning
little by little to the anemone,
until into her lap the loud heavens
pour their polyphonic light,

muscle of endless receiving
tense in the unmoving starlike flower,
sometimes so overcharged with fullness
that the call of dusk to rest

is scarcely able to bargain back
the petals, so widely open are they:
you, perseverance and strength from how many worlds!

We, who are destroyers, go on much longer.
But when, in which of our lives,
are we at last open and receiving?

II,6

Rose, sovereign flower, to those in ancient times
you were a cup with a single rim
but for us you are the many-petalled bloom,
the inexhaustible other.

In your abundance you shine like silk on silk
wrapped round a centre holding only light;
nonetheless one of your petals by itself
is at the same time the refusal and denial of any show.

For centuries your perfume has been calling
its sweetest names over to us,
suddenly it fills the air like fame.

Even so we can't possess it quite, we guess…
and memory jumps across to it,
which we have begged from countless uncalled hours.

II,7

Flowers, kin in the end to hands which are your guide,
(to the hands of girls from now and from the past),
you who have lain on garden tables, often from edge
to edge, wilting and gently hurting,

waiting for water, so that death, already
within you, might be postponed – , and now
taken up again between the streaming fingertips
of touching hands, which, more than you might have guessed,

are able to restore your better health,
provided you are given time to revive in a vase,
slowly becoming cooler: and the girl's warmth leaving you

like a confession, like a dull discolouring sin
committed when you were picked, yet linking
you back to these your friends who also bloom.

II,8

You few, the playmates of my vanished childhood
in the scattered gardens of the city:
how we used to meet and timidly amuse each other
and like the story-book lamb with words in a scroll,

speak while being silent. And if we were suddenly happy
at the same time, no one possessed it. Whose could it possibly be?
How it melted away among the bustling people
among the fears of the long following year.

Unfamiliar carriages rolled past us, sometimes swerving near,
tall houses overlooked us, but quite unseeing – not a soul
knew us. Was anything real in the world?

Nothing. Only the balls we threw, their imperishable flight.
Not even the children... though sometimes one would step,
ah, so fleetingly, under the plunging ball.

In memoriam Egon von Rilke

II,9

Law-givers, do not boast that you have dispensed
with torture and the use of iron shackles.
A willed spasm of mercy may convulse you
and yet not cause a change of heart.

What is reprieved by fashion, will later go to the scaffold
by default, like a child's cast-off toys
from last year's birthday. Into the pure, high,
and wide open heart the god of real mercy

would enter differently. He would strike like
lightning and radiate might as only a god can do.
More than a wind for great stately ships,

and not less than the tender wordless understanding
that silently spreads through us from our depths
as through a child quietly playing in the lap of nature.

II,10

All that has been gained the machine threatens, so long
as it seeks to direct rather than serve.
Lest it be slowed down by the sweet embellishments of
                                        the craftman's hand
it cuts the stone straighter for our unsmiling buildings.

Never does it rest, being oiled in some quiet workshop,
and allow us to draw level while it is restored to itself.
Indeed it is alive, – thinks that it knows what is best,
with an unwavering purpose orders and makes and destroys.

But for us life is still full of mystery, and in a hundred places
is beginning afresh. A drama of pure forces,
no one is touched who does not kneel and wonder.

Words gently go their way before the unsayable…
and music, always new, out of the most resonant stones
builds in unusable space her god revealing house.

II,11

Many a neat and tidy rule of death took root,
law-making man, because you continued to hunt,
but I understand better than traps or nets, that strip of canvas
they used to hang down into the caves in the Karst.

Gently they unwound you, as if you were a token of peace.
But then at the mouth the helper gave you a twist,
– and out of the cave, the darkness tossed a handful of pigeons,
pale and groggy, flapping towards the light… but this too is right.

Let the onlooker be untouched by pity,
not only the hunter who, sharp-eyed and quick-witted,
must finish the task.

Killing is a form of our wandering sorrow…
pure is the cheerful spirit
and even so are we.

II,12

Seek renewal. Be inspired by fire, the flame
which, though flaunting its changes, cannot be held down:
the fashioning spirit, which orders earthly matters,
loves most in the living form its air of leaving.

Whatever clings to the past is already stiffening,
does it think itself safe by turning an inconspicuous grey?
Wait, from afar what is hardest warns all those less hard.
Beware – an absent hammer is being raised.

He who lets himself flow like spring water, him knowledge knows;
enthralled, he is led by it through the joyful world,
which repeatedly ends with a beginning and begins with an end.

Every happy space is a child or a grandchild of parting,
through which they walk astonished. And Daphne transfigured,
feeling herself become laurel, requires you to change into a wind.

II,13

Be ahead of all leaving as though it were behind you
like the winter, which is now relenting.
For among winters there is one, which is so endless,
that only by outwintering it does the heart survive.

Be dead for ever in Eurydice and rise more strongly singing,
more strongly praising, back in pure accord.
Here in their faded company, in the unlit kingdom,
be a shivering glass, carry death in your ringing.

Be – and in the same breath know not-being,
infinite ground of your recurring strength,
that you inhabit fully this one time.

To the blunted and stifled masses of teeming Nature
as well as to the spent, to the unthinkable sum
jubilantly add yourself, then destroy the score.

II,14

Look at the flowers, these cut ones, true to their earthly origin,
to whom we lend a fate from the edge of our fate, –
yet without even noticing it! If they regret their dying,
surely it should fall to us to be their sorrow.

All things want to be joyful. But here we travel
weighed down by our self-importance;
O what dreary teachers we are of nature,
while she quite simply lives in endless childhood.

If someone took what is real into innermost sleep
and dwelt there with it deeply, O how lightly he would rise,
another person to another day, out of the common depths.

Or he might stay perhaps, and they would grow and praise him,
now so changed that he is closer to them,
the quiet sisters and brothers of windy meadows.

II,15

O fountain mouth, provider, fluent source
of unrehearsed pure speech, tell, –
you who hide the water's restless face
behind your marble mask. And further off

the guiding aqueduct. Thus from the distance,
past the burial grounds, down the Apennine
slopes is brought your story to babble
out over your blackened chin

into the basin lying here beneath.
This is the attentive ear laid down in sleep,
the marble ear in which you always whisper.

The hollow ear of the earth. And this is how she
listens to herself. If you plunge in a pitcher
it will seem to her as if you interrupt.

II,16

Again and again we have torn apart
the god whose place is to heal.
We are restless because we want to know,
while he is calm and composed.

Even the most precious gift
passes into his world without comment,
and at the proffered end
he looks on without moving.

When the god has signalled,
the dead will drink from the spring,
which we on earth only hear.

To us, just the sound is carried.
And the lamb who begs for his bell
does so from a surer instinct.

II,17

Where, in which forever happy gardens,
on which trees, and from which denuded blossoms,
do the strange fruit of consolation ripen? Those
refreshing fruit, one of which you will happen on perhaps

in the trampled meadow of your need.
From one find to the next, you wonder at the size,
soundness, and softness of the skin,
and that a bird's quickness or worm's persistence

did not bring it there first. Can there be trees, visited
by angels, and raised so strangely by patient unseen gardeners,
that they offer us their fruit, without their being ours?

And have we never had the power, we shades and ciphers,
not through our boisterous prime or sudden fading,
to trouble the measured calm of those long summers?

II,18

Dancer: you who change fleetingness
into measure: see how you have succeeded!
And the pirouette at the close, that whirling tree,
perhaps it has gathered all of your growing year.

The tip of the tree that a moment ago was swaying,
hasn't it now into stillness suddenly entered?
And above it, wasn't there sun, wasn't there summer,
the warmth, that immeasurable warmth coming from you?

They were fruitful as well, bore fruit, your jubilant branches,
for aren't these their gifts: the jug streaked
with ripeness, the vase even riper still?

And in the sketches: doesn't the stroke continue
what the dark slash of your eyebrow
drew on the wall of your own swift spin?

II,19

Somewhere gold lives in the sumptuous bank
and takes its ease with all the paper thousands. And yet
that blind beggar is like a bare patch of land or dusty
space under a cupboard, unvisited by even copper coins.

In the smart high streets money is quite at home
and can be seen dressed up as buttonhole, silk and fur.
But in the pause between the breaths of all the groaning money,
waking or sleeping, stands the silent god.

How the eternally outstretched hand would like to rest.
But in the morning fate drags it back, and day after day
holds it out: empty, wretched and weak.

Perhaps one day, someone who sees deeply will understand
and praise need's constant presence. Sayable
only in song. To be heeded only by a god.

II,20

What vast distances between the stars; but nevertheless
how much more we learn from what is close to hand.
Somebody, a child for example, and nearby somebody else,
and yet how inconceivably far off.

Fate measures us, perhaps, by the scope of being,
which seems to be alien to us;
think only of how far it is from a woman to a man
when she both likes and shuns him.

Everything is open – nowhere does the circle close.
Look into the dish, on the table laid for a meal,
at the curious face of a fish.

Fishes are dumb… one supposes. But who knows?
For in the end isn't there a place where what would be
the language of fishes is spoken even without them?

II,21

Sing, my heart, of gardens, sing what you do not know,
distant, unclouded gardens, shining like polished stone,
water and perfumed roses of Ispahan or Shiraz,
joyfully sing them, praise them, in their loveliness unsurpassed.

Show, my heart, that you never miss them,
that they dream you, their ripening figs.
That you know their blossoming branches
on your face as a strengthening breeze.

And never for a moment suppose
something lost, since you chose this: your path!
Silk thread you are part of the tapestry.

From images which deeply connect you,
(one or many from this life of pain),
know the whole sublime pattern intended.

II,22

O despite fate: the magnificent abundance
of our being, brimming over in parks, –
or as men of stone next to
high thresholds, shouldering balconies.

O the brazen bell that every day
clangs out against the dull routine.
Or the single column in Karnak, the column
that outlasted the almost indestructible temples.

But now these same exuberant forms come crashing down
as pure dispatch out of the even yellow day
into an emphatic night shot through with light.

And the rage melts away without a trace.
Just curves of flight through the air and what was pulled after,
nothing perhaps in vain. Yet only as held dear.

II,23

Call me to that one among your hours,
which you are never quite able to possess,
close and imploring like a dog's face
but then escaped from you

just when you thought to have grasped it.
This though is what is most yours.
We are free. There we were dismissed,
at the very place we expected to be greeted.

Fearful, we long for our balance,
yet sometimes we're too young for what is old
and too old for what never has been.

Even so, our role is to praise,
for, alas, we are both bough and axe,
and the sweetness of ripening danger.

II,24

O this delight, forever fresh, out of the ploughed earth!
Although there was no help for the first adventurers,
cities sprang up all the same on favoured seaboards,
jug and barrel were filled with water and oil.

We give the gods pride of place in our daring plans,
which sullen fate brings to nought by way of return.
But they abide. And we may sense their presence
but they too in the end acknowledge us.

We, a family of a thousand years: mothers and fathers
again and again completed by the future child,
who some day struggles higher and takes them by surprise.

We, so endlessly ventured, how much time we have!
And only silent death can know what we are
and what he yet will gather when he lets us be.

II,25

Listen, already you can hear the first rakes
working the soil; the return of human effort
to the retentive silence of the rich early
Spring earth. Their presence seems to have

all its own vigour. What has happened
so many times before, still contrives to come
as something new. You always longed for Spring
yet never grasped it. Rather it took hold of you.

Although some oak tree leaves have come through winter
they seem in the dusk to hint at their turning brown.
Sometimes the breezes exchange faint signs of life.

The undergrowth is black. But piles of manure
stand a much deeper black in the fields close by.
Every hour that passes proves to be younger.

II,26

How the shriek of a bird will shake us…
any cry once it has broken in.
And again children at play in the open
cry far beyond their actual cries.

Cry correspondence. Into the many breaches
within the one space, (where birdsong
plunges entire, as people into dreams)
they dart their piercing shouts.

Where, O where can we be? Ever more free,
like kites torn loose from the earth
we swoop in the air with rippling laughter,

buffeted by the wind. Gather these shrill ones up,
O singing God! Let them awaken trembling,
bearing within them like a tide the head and the lyre.

II,27

Does time ever build, time the destroyer?
When will it strike the castle on the peaceful mountain?
And when will this heart, which belongs utterly
to the gods, be torn apart by their might?

Are we really so wretchedly weak
as fate comes to make us believe?
Is childhood: profound, full of promise,
at its roots – in its growing – sterile?

Ah, how the ghost of change
slips through our trusting openness
as though it were nothing but smoke.

Nevertheless, as what we are, the resolute,
we have a place near the abiding
powers, as godlike practice.

II,28

O come and go. You, almost still a child,
reconcile for an instant the dance's pattern
with the starry heavens, that private rapture
through which we may, though fleetingly, surpass

dull lawful nature. For she herself was raised
only to absolute hearing when Orpheus sang.
You were still at that sound quickened
and easily astonished, as when a tree delayed

from going with you into the listening ear.
And still you knew the place from where the lyre
created its own sound, the witheld centre.

For nature's sake you tested graceful steps
and hoped one day to turn the face and actions
of him, your friend, towards the healing rite.

II,29

Silent friend of many distances, feel
how your breath enlarges even space.
Beneath the timbers of gloomy belfries
let yourself be rung. Air which feeds on you

grows vigorous from this fare.
Through the exchange toll yourself back and forth.
What is the deepest suffering you have known?
Is drinking bitter to you, turn into wine?

In the darkest part of the night's depth,
at the mysterious crossroad of the senses,
be the intention of their strange encounter.

And if through daily use you are forgotten,
to the still earth whisper: I flow.
To the rushing waters say: I am.

Notes on *The Sonnets to Orpheus*

Part One

Sonnet 1

The opening poem is a myth of origins. Orpheus is moved to song by his experience of a tree standing towering above him and the sound of the breeze in its leaves and branches. He identifies with it and through so doing his song comes to represent the tree, and he becomes self-conscious. The phrase 'tall tree in the ear' together with similar phrases in I,2 and II,28 might be regarded as a description of the auditory imagination. However, in view of the description of 'world-space' being unified through hearing in II,26, Rilke is perhaps suggesting that hearing provides a privileged path to an experience of oneness between what is celebrated in song and the song itself. The holding back, the ability to reflect on the experience of primal oneness, rather than make immediate responses, opens up a sense of inner space within Orpheus. He is able to transmit this feeling of inwardness to the animals through the taming power of his song which compels their attention. Their ability to listen is described in terms that suggest the anatomy of the middle and inner ear.

Sonnet 2

Because of his sensitivity to song the poet becomes aware of a young girl. She is in some respects the creation of Orpheus, and she becomes the counterpart of the poet because she contains everything that has stirred his wonder. The poet questions Orpheus on how he so perfects or completes his creation by turning her away from life. The questions 'Where is her death?' and 'Where does she fall from me?' suggest that the poet struggles to know whether the girl has a real existence or is a creation of his own imagination. She is his muse and in these poems Vera Ouckama Knoop is her embodiment. The tragedy of premature death, which so haunted Rilke, is implicit in this poem.

Sonnet 3

In the imagery of these poems, Orpheus can pass through the lyre as a gateway to the eternal realm of the dead. The time-rooted nature of desire and possession are of no concern to the god. In order to be a great poet, love of the phenomenal world is insufficient, beauty must be loved in full appreciation of its relationship to eternity.

Sonnet 4

Key words in the sequence, Atem (breath), Luft (breeze) and Raum (space) appear for the first time in this poem. Inspiration, openness to experience, creativity and life itself are balanced against suffering, loss and death.

Sonnet 5

The rose becomes here an emblem of Orpheus. Even though we sometimes lose our sense of his involvement in human life, the rose is a reminder of his abiding interest.

The rose has always been a symbol of femininity to Rilke and perhaps this implies an androgynous quality to Orpheus.

Sonnet 8

A myth created by Rilke in which rejoicing, longing and sorrow are described as 'sisters of the heart'. In an untitled poem ('Für Leonie Zacharias') written in 1921 Rilke writes that the role of the poet is to praise, and in this poem that grief may only be expressed within the wider context of affirmation.

Sonnet 11

This poem is about rapport and intimacy, in this case between horse and rider. It is suggested that there is something which resists analysis in perfect understanding between individuals, although doubt is also cast on whether this is possible despite the power of the image of unity.

Sonnet 17

The world tree connects the three realms of the underworld, earth and heavens, or the unconscious, daily life and the imagination. The poet/hero climbs the tree, passing the breakable (mortal) branches, which are limited by conting-ency, on his ascent. By becoming the still growing topmost branch he achieves absolute freedom and immortality. The identification of the poet with Orpheus is complete.

Sonnet 18

A new theme, that of industrialisation, is introduced. Hearing or sensibility is damaged by the noise of the machines. There is a concern that machines will control us rather than we them.

Sonnet 20

As is made clear in a letter to Lou Andreas-Salomé on 11th February 1922 this poem recalls a horse they saw together on one of their visits to Russia over twenty years previously.

Sonnet 24

A warning that the pace of life in an industrial society alienates us from nature and from each other.

Sonnet 25

The first poem in the sequence directly to commemorate Vera Ouckama Knoop. The mystery, horror and devastation of sudden major illness is described. In one of his few notes accompanying the poems Rilke records that this poem is 'To Vera'.

Sonnet 26

The final poem of the first part of *Sonnets to Orpheus* suggests that it was only through his physical destruction that Orpheus was able to transmit his gifts of listening and music making.

Notes on *The Sonnets to Orpheus*

Part Two

Sonnet 1
A meditation on breathing. Through inspiration and expiration the poet is placed in a dynamic relationship with the world – 'Single wave whose swelling sea I am.' A deep connectedness and harmony is implied.

Sonnet 3
This poem analyses a sequence of events with great precision. The girl looks attentively at her reflection, and sees the reflection as beautiful. This causes a change in the way she feels about herself and this alters her appearance. This in turn passes to the mirror where it is seen as height-ened self-consciousness and self-possession. There is then a further adjustment of her self-regard.

The empty holes in sieves exist only by virtue of what lies outside them, and the same is true of the reflection in the mirror. Nevertheless the poem shows that there is a genuine dynamic between the girl and her image, which mimics and externalizes the movements of introspection. Rilke uses the word Zwischenraüme (intervals) in this poem and again in II,26. I will discuss its use further in the note to that poem.

Sonnet 4
The unicorn is both a creation of the imagination and a symbol of it. The awakening of the girl, though sexual, is also gentle and dream-like.

Sonnet 6

The rose had already been the subject of poems by Rilke, of which the most elaborate was 'Die Rosenschale' ('The Rose Bowl') published in *Neue Gedichte*. Rilke associated the rose with femininity, receptivity and interiority.

The conclusion of this poem probably owes something to a paragraph in an essay by Proust entitled 'On Reading', which was first published in 1905 and later as an introduction to a translation of Ruskin's *Sesame and Lilies*. The passage I have in mind refers to the sentences and the intervals between them which for Proust summon up the forms of the ancient soul. Writing of St. Luke's Gospel and the canticle-like passages which follow the pauses after colons, Proust hears the silence of the worshipper. He then adds 'this silence still filled the pause in the sentence which having been divided so as to enclose it, had preserved the form of it; and more than once as I read, it brought to me the scent of a rose which the breeze entering through the open window had spread through the upper room where the gathering was being held and which had not evaporated in almost two thousand years.'

In the last years of his life Rilke composed a number of short French poems, *Les Roses*, as well as his epitaph:

> Rose, oh reiner Widerspruch, Lust,
> Niemandes Schlaf zu sein unter soviel
> Lidern.

> Rose, oh pure contradiction, delight,
> at being nobody's sleep under so many
> eyelids.

There are puns on reiner/Rainer (pure/his name) and Lidern/
Liedern (eyelids/songs) which cannot be rendered in English.

Sonnet 7
A tour de force. The only sonnet which is one uninterrupted
sentence.

Sonnet 8
An evocation of Rilke's childhood in Prague. It is dedicated
to the memory of his cousin Egon with whom Rilke played
as a child and who died at a young age.

Sonnet 9
The fashionable liberal measures of politicians are compared
to the absent-minded reprieve of old toys which sooner or
later will be thrown away. Real mercy requires an open and
loving heart.

Sonnet 10
The poem returns to the subject matter of I,18 and the fear
that machines will disrupt our relationship with nature.

Sonnet 11
Rilke describes a hunting practice in the limestone caves
around Trieste. Although he has stated that above all the task
of the poet is to praise, it is difficult not to feel that he is
gently ridiculing the hunters.

Sonnet 12
The theme of renewal will be continued into the next poem.

A powerful, almost apocalyptic image of an absent hammer which will shatter everything that resists change, is perhaps simply the passage of time.

Sonnet 13

Rilke wrote to Gertrud Ouckama Knoop on 18th March 1922 enclosing a copy of this one poem, 'because it is the closest to me of the whole series and the most important one in it.' (He had previously written to her twice in February after the first part of *Sonnets to Orpheus* had been completed and sent copies of all twenty-six of the poems.)

'Be ahead of all leaving' does not imply that one should avoid the pain of loss by anticipating it. Rather it indicates that by having already registered the agony of loss to its utmost degree, one is then able to continue to engage with life, affirm it and press forward. The poet, like Orpheus, must renounce the beloved and return 'more strongly praising.' Pater's celebrated remarks at the end of his book, *The Renaissance*, provide a partial commentary on this and the preceding poem. 'A counted number of pulses only is given to us of a variegated, dramatic life. How may we see in them all that is to be seen in them by the finest senses? How shall we pass most swiftly from point to point, and be present always at the focus where the greatest number of vital forces unite in their purest energy? To burn always with this hard, gem-like flame, to maintain this ecstasy, is success in life.' He adds that the formation of habits lessens this ability to feel intensely. This passage is almost a mission statement for aestheticism and was enormously influential in its time. However, in Rilke, as in Keats, the aptitude for intense feeling is built more explicitly on the ever-present awareness of absolute loss and indeed grows directly out of it.

Sonnet 18
The content of this poem is informed by the correspondence with Vera's mother in the weeks before these poems were written. At the end of her life, when she was unable to dance, Vera painted pictures.

Sonnet 20
Rilke describes the incalculable inner spaces within people which make mutual understanding and intimacy so difficult. The last three lines are obscure, but seem to suggest a Platonic realm where there is an ideal record of everything.

Sonnet 21
The affirmative tone is hard won but, despite that, loss is described as in some sense illusory. There is a triumphant conclusion which asserts that we must trust in the meaning of the pattern even if we are unable to make it out or understand its significance.

Sonnet 23
In his note to this sonnet, Rilke wrote that this poem was addressed 'To the Reader.' This puts one in mind of Baudelaire's opening poem in *Les Fleurs du Mal*, also addressed 'To the Reader'. There Baudelaire describes extreme feelings of boredom which amount to self-loathing and to which he himself is prey. However, he insists that they are familiar to his readers as well. In this poem, after the first

six lines in which Orpheus addresses the reader, Rilke speaks for himself and us through the remaining eight lines, attributing feelings to us which we may not immediately wish to acknowledge as our own. I take it that the sonnet refers to the moments of sexual ecstasy. A homely image, the muzzle of a dog, which if grasped pulls away and out of the hand, is likened to the sensation of orgasm. (There is also an anatomical appropriateness to the image.) The strength and vividness of the climax inexorably ebbs away again without of itself offering any sense of communion. This is a more complex variation on the theme of 'post coitum omne animal triste.'

Lines 9-11 are difficult. The anti-climax is disorientating. We are too ignorant or inexperienced to understand why the ecstasy of orgasm fades away inconclusively, despite the fact that it was ever thus. We are too much creatures of our kind to transform orgasm into a path to revelation.

Perhaps the suggestion of the conclusion is that through experiencing extinction (*la petite mort*) more completely in orgasm, the individual may return to life more fully as well. Herein is the sweetness of approaching danger. There is some support for this interpretation in the 'Worker Letter' which was written only days before this poem and in which sexual ecstasy is described as being focused on the genitals rather than experienced all over the body.

Sonnet 26
This poem recalls a time in a garden in Capri described in the prose piece 'Experience' ('Erlebnis'). 'A bird call in the open and in his consciousness was one, when it did not, as it

were, break on the barrier of his body but gathered both together in undivided space, in which there was only one region of purest deepest consciousness, mysteriously protected. On that occasion he had closed his eyes so that he might not be confused by the contour of the body in such a generously granted experience, and infinity passed into him from all sides in so familiar a manner that he believed he felt within him the gentle presence of the stars which had now appeared.'

In the lines 5-6, conscious beings are described as breaches (Zwischenraüme) in worldspace (Weltraum), a phrase which hints at the mystery of selfhood. But there is also the suggestion that the breach may be annulled by the shrillness of birdsong or the cry of a child which awakens some echo or correspondence in us. The prose passage adds that through some obscure attunement of inner and outer an oceanic state of feeling may arise, while the poem goes on to liken us in our oneness with the open to kites in the wind. As mentioned in the note to Sonnet II,3 Rilke also uses the word Zwischenraüme in the poem about mirrors, but there refers to gaps or intervals in time. In this poem by contrast the cries of birds and children are breaches in space not time. I do not think it puts too great a burden of interpret - ation on the two poems to see a parallel with Kant's inner sense (time) and outer sense (space). Although the image in the mirror falls on outer sense, the reflection disturbs the girl's experience of herself. There is a breach in personal time or inner sense at the instant of altered self-awareness. So Rilke suggests in these two poems that each private world of consciousness is discontinuous with the outer world, but continuous with itself in time. As a breach in world space, a person is separated from others and constantly engaged in the effort of establishing relatedness. Sometimes a moment of attunement, correspondence or coincidence may afford a brief feeling of oneness with the outer world. As an uninterrupted line of world time, an individual may be shocked or jolted into feeling things differently. A change of awareness of the self will be seeded between a hitherto undifferentiated before and after, so that the passage of time is experienced as a development or even a crisis.

Why does individual experience have the properties of being separate from the external world in space and continuous with itself in time? Consider: if self-conscious beings were seamlessly wedded to the material world, it would be impossible to assign any role to consciousness whatsoever. And if beings were recreated anew in every moment there would be no historical self in which to anchor experience.

Sonnet 28

Like the penultimate poem in the first part, Rilke noted that this poem was 'To Vera'.

There is the suggestion that Vera, through her dance, is able to heal nature, which raises her to an archetypal level as a benefactor or even saviour of humankind. There also seems to be a problem, perhaps the approach of illness, when the harmony between Vera and nature is disrupted, 'as when a tree delayed from going with you into the listening ear.' The translation of 'die unerhörte Mitte' is difficult and unsatisfactory. It is more than the unheard centre, but unheard of centre which is perhaps the nearest one can come to a literal translation, has unwanted connotations in English. The meaning seems to be that the existence of the centre is inaudible to mortals and therefore its existence unsuspected by them.

Sonnet 29
Rilke's note to this poem says 'To a friend of Vera' and refers of course to himself.

It is a poem about transformation. The 'mysterious crossroad of the senses' is a place of synaesthesia and illumination. The riddle of self, both substance and process, is analogous to the particle/wave duality of quantum physics. But the final assertion is of the individual's irreducible substantiality.

APPENDIX

Rainer Maria Rilke

SKETCHES FROM TWO WINTER EVENINGS

Translated by David Cook

Prelude

Why do I suddenly see the park fountain
framed beneath the roof of elms?
The water in the old basin
is like the background of a portrait.

I was drawn to it. Perhaps before that I saw
the possibility of the softest oval.
Was it the hope of a Kashmir shawl
which I lost against the reflected leaves?

Who can tell, now that youth no longer deceives?
How many attempts to grasp absence
has pure water wonderfully chastened;
and yet it still shines up, nourishing the dream?

I

Nothing has stayed so beautiful. But then I was too small.
It was afternoon. Suddenly they wanted to dance
and without pausing rolled back the carpet from the floor.
(What a shimmering light still lies upon the scene!)

And then they danced. I saw but her alone,
though sometimes I would lose her
because that scent of hers had become the world
and I was drowning in it. I was too small.

But could I ever even when full-grown
have become the master of such a thrilling perfume,
and thus been able to force myself
out of that clinging aura like a stone?

No, nothing so beautiful. Her flower-laden scent
in that garden room on that day so long ago.
It is intact. Cannot be gainsaid.
And it is mine. Unending benediction.

This is rapture: what flew over us
the possibility of happiness. No, not quite that.
Impossibility even; simply an assumption
that this one summer, this one garden room, –
that the tinkling minutes' music
was innocent, since it beguiled us chastely.

And you, even then grown-up, how I think of you!
No longer as I did, as an anxious child,
but almost like a god, taking his pleasure.
For when these hours stretch onward without end
perhaps we may be granted such a life
as to build directly out of scent and light.

Everything is dear to me, your freckles
and the clasp which fastened your sleeve;
oh how overwhelming and undiminished
is that sweetness which never cloys.

I stood there reeling, bursting
with the fullness of my heart,
in my childish fingers, half crumpled
a convolvulus flower. –

Oh how life, just beginning to strengthen,
wishes to exalt what is adored,
but from its own self-doubt
hangs down as from a garden wall.

No, I'll not forget you
        however much I change,
lovely early light
        firstborn of Earth.

All that you prefigured
	has in time been given,
for you broke my heart
	open without force.

Most fleeting, foremost figure
	by whom I was awakened:
now I've grown strong
	I praise tenderness.

That I wrote about fruit
follows perhaps from your bending
to gather strawberries;
and if flowers don't fade in me,
isn't that because happiness moved you
to pick one?

I remember how you ran
and suddenly, short of breath,
turned towards me and waited.
I sat by your side as you slept;
your left hand
lay like a rose.

Did I ever escape your early influence?
Aren't you on every path
always ahead of me and in command;
when might we ever become equal?

You were so direct, not even the stylishness
of your clothes made me self-conscious.
How your sudden leaving is a part of me... will
it dwindle away with my death?

Or might I, as a refutation of my own demise,
throw your influence back onto Nature?
the long agitation
in your pursuit?

This too is possible: to say: No.
And to stick stubbornly with the boys;
for fear of exaggerating
the impression made by a girl.

Will the young men prove equal
to so gentle a power?
Alas even friends remain obscure,
wholly unattainable.

Let tenderness and hardness silently test you.
Some who softly come to meet you
will bless you, beyond expectation.
Yes, they will bless you.

II

How did it happen? To succeed in loving,
when at school nothing succeeded!
The infinite is forever unknowable
between rising and setting.

In him silently it came to pass,
whose mouth was too young to find words,
but whose heart travelled the sweep
of the inexpressible love-year.

What were mealtimes, school, ballgames, punishment,
what was waking, what sleeping?
Here in steeply ordered octaves
the whole future sounded as one.

So even then it was tasted,
and his heart gained the upper hand, –
while the life, still immature,
stood aloof from boyish games.

At the time too much had been given,
and thus his future shaped;
later life would measure him, –
there it reached out and took hold.

For the god, hidden from the woman,
felt himself whole in this child,
here, in the boy's defeat
he rooted the endurance of the man.

Note on *Sketches from Two Winter Evenings*

This poem was dedicated to his publisher Anton
Kippenberg and dated 22 May 1924. It is an extraordinary autobiographical fragment, although I know
of no identification of the young woman described.
I would hazard a guess that Rilke is about 8 or 9 years
old and the woman 22 or 23, but this is based entirely
on the text of the poem. Rilke tells us that the effect
this woman had on him was so profound that it
prefigured his whole life as a poet. From a number of
sources, though principally his own writings, we have
a picture of Rilke, the child, as lonely, bewildered,
anxious, neglected and at times subject to the terror
of feeling abandoned. He wrote that he felt adults
were unreliable, expressing an interest in him and
then disappearing. Sadly this happened again in this
encounter at a somewhat older age, but even if it is 'a
screen memory' it stands out as enormously
significant because he looks back with joy and
gratitude to this young woman who was kind to him.
For a very brief period, Rilke experienced rapture and
the feeling lit up his unhappy life for the following
year. But there is also a quality of his being haunted,
so that he writes 'Aren't you on every path always
ahead of me and in command' and astonishingly
'How your sudden leaving is a part of me… will it
dwindle away with my death?' This of course is like
the loss of Eurydice by Orpheus and somehow, out of

the disaster, the poet must find the strength and the voice to praise. All these years later Rilke sees that it is he not the woman who is extraordinary, 'For the god, hidden from the woman, felt himself whole in this child.' At this late stage of his life, Rilke is able to understand that the beloved is at least in part the creation of the beholder of beauty.

The lines 'Or might I, as a refutation of my own demise, throw your influence back onto Nature?' seem particularly obscure and I find them oddly troubling. It is as though 'the witheld centre' ('die unerhörte Mitte') of *Sonnets to Orpheus* II,28 were the androgynous immortal heart of our being, which might only be broached when all projections are cast off.